The School Bus

by Meg Michael
illustrated by Kersti Frigell

 SRA
McGraw-Hill

Columbus, Ohio

A Division of The **McGraw·Hill** *Companies*

SRA/McGraw-Hill

A Division of The McGraw·Hill Companies

Copyright © 1998 by SRA/McGraw-Hill.

Printed in the United States of America.

Send all inquiries to:
SRA/McGraw-Hill
250 Old Wilson Bridge Road
Suite 310
Worthington, OH 43085

ISBN 0-02-674312-4
  2 3 4 5 6 7 8 9 SEG 00 99 98 97

Here Comes the Bus

Do not fuss!
Pick up your stuff.
Here comes the bus.

Slip on your mittens.
Where is your hat?

Do you have your bag?
Don't forget that.

Zip up your jacket.
Tuck a scarf on your neck.

Pick up your hat.
Put it on your head.

Oh no, here it comes!
You must run to the stop.

Here is your bag.
Just get to that stop.

On the bus, there is a bad smell.

10

What is that smell?
We can not tell.

Sniff, sniff. Whiff, whiff.
What is that stuff?

The bus man smells it
and stops the bus.

13

Look at Russ.
Russ is the one.
In his box there is a bun.

14

On the bun is something
that smells.
Dump that bun, Russ,
and all will be well.

Here, Russ. This is for you.
You can have what we have, too.